AUTONOMY

Navigating the Complexities of the Mind

By Saba Isah

Table of contents

➢ <u>Definition of mental health</u>

Mental health refers to a person's overall psychological and emotional well-being. It includes the ability to manage one's thoughts, emotions, and behaviors, to cope with stress and challenges, to form and maintain healthy relationships, and to make decisions that promote well-being. Mental health is not just the absence of mental illness or disorder, but rather a positive state of mind and a sense of resilience in the face of life's challenges. It can be influenced by a variety of factors, including genetics, environment, lifestyle, and life experiences. Good mental health is essential for living a fulfilling and productive life.

Mental health encompasses emotional, psychological, and social well-being, influencing cognition, perception, and behavior. It likewise determines how an individual handles stress, interpersonal relationships, and decision-making.

Mental health includes subjective well-being, perceived self-efficacy, autonomy, competence, intergenerational dependence, and self-actualization of one's intellectual and emotional potential, among others. From the perspectives of positive psychology or holism, mental health may include an individual's ability to enjoy life and to create a balance between life activities and efforts to achieve psychological resilience. Cultural differences, subjective assessments, and competing professional theories all affect how one defines "mental health". Some early signs related to mental health difficulties are sleep irritation, lack of energy, lack of appetite and thinking of harming yourself or others.

Mental health is a state of emotional, psychological, and social well-being in which individuals are able to cope with the normal stresses of life, work productively, and make positive contributions to their communities. It involves the ability to manage one's thoughts, feelings, and behaviors in a way that promotes a sense of inner peace, self-esteem, and resilience in the face of adversity. Good mental health allows individuals to form and maintain meaningful relationships, pursue their goals and interests, and navigate the complexities of life with confidence and optimism. It is an integral part of overall health and well-being, and is influenced by a range of factors such as genetics, environment, and life experiences. Maintaining good mental health requires ongoing self-care, support from others, and access to appropriate resources and treatments when needed.

➢ <u>Differentiating between mental health and mental illness</u>

Mental health, as defined by the Public Health Agency of Canada, is an individual's capacity to feel, think, and act in ways to achieve a better quality of life while respecting the personal, social, and cultural boundaries. Impairment of any of these are risk factors for mental disorders, or mental illnesses, which are a component of mental health. Mental disorders are defined as the health conditions that affect and alter cognitive functioning, emotional responses, and behavior associated with distress and/or impaired functioning. The ICD-11 is the global standard used to diagnose, treat, research, and report various mental disorders. In the United States, the DSM-5 is used as the classification system of mental disorders.

While mental health and mental disorders are often used interchangeably, there are significant differences between the two. Mental health is a positive state of well-being that allows an individual to cope with the challenges of life, while mental disorders are characterized by significant disturbances in an individual's thoughts, emotions, or behaviors that impair their functioning.

Mental health refers to a state of well-being in which an individual is able to cope with the normal stresses of life, work productively, and contribute to their community. Mental health is not just the absence of mental illness; it encompasses a range of positive factors, such as emotional resilience, positive relationships, and the ability to adapt to change.

Mental disorders, on the other hand, are conditions that affect an individual's thinking, behavior, or emotions. Mental disorders are characterized by significant distress, impairment, or dysfunction in one or more areas of an individual's life. Mental disorders can range from mild to severe and can have a significant impact on an individual's quality of life.

While mental health and mental disorders are distinct concepts, they are closely related. Good mental health can protect against the development of mental disorders, while individuals with mental disorders can benefit from efforts to improve their mental health.

It is important to note that mental health and mental disorders are not static concepts. Mental health can fluctuate over time, and individuals may experience mental health challenges at different points in their lives. Similarly, mental disorders can be treated and managed, and individuals with mental disorders can recover and experience good mental health.

❖ <u>The impact of mental health on overall well-being</u>

Mental health has a significant impact on an individual's overall well-being. Mental health and well-being are closely interconnected, and good mental health is essential for achieving and maintaining a positive sense of well-being.

Here are some ways in which mental health impacts well-being:

1. **Emotional well-being:** Mental health affects emotional well-being by influencing an individual's ability to manage their emotions and cope with stress. Good mental health can help individuals to develop resilience and maintain a positive outlook, which can enhance emotional well-being.

Emotional well-being refers to the ability to understand and manage one's emotions in a positive and constructive way. It is a key component of overall well-being and is essential for a fulfilling and meaningful life.

Characteristics of emotional well-being:

- Self-awareness: Emotional well-being requires a high degree of self-awareness, which involves recognizing and understanding one's own emotions, as well as their impact on oneself and others.

- Emotional regulation: Emotional well-being also involves the ability to regulate one's emotions effectively, which means being able to manage negative emotions and express positive emotions in a healthy and constructive way.

- Resilience: Emotional well-being requires resilience, which involves the ability to bounce back from setbacks and challenges, and to maintain a positive outlook even in difficult circumstances.

- Empathy: Emotional well-being also involves empathy, which means being able to understand and respond to the emotions of others in a sensitive and supportive way.

- Positive relationships: Emotional well-being is closely linked to positive relationships, which involve open and honest communication, mutual respect, and a sense of trust and connection.

In summary, emotional well-being is essential for overall well-being and involves self-awareness, emotional regulation, resilience, empathy, and positive relationships. By prioritizing emotional well-being, individuals can develop the skills and habits necessary to manage their emotions effectively and lead a fulfilling and meaningful life.

2. **Physical well-being:** Mental health also has an impact on physical well-being. Mental health conditions such as depression and anxiety can contribute to physical health problems such as insomnia, fatigue, and chronic pain.

Physical well-being refers to the state of being in good physical health, which involves having a healthy body, a balanced diet, regular exercise, and adequate rest. Physical well-being is an important component of overall well-being, as it affects an individual's ability to engage in daily activities and pursue their goals and interests.

factors that contribute to physical well-being:

- Physical health: Good physical health involves maintaining a healthy body, including having healthy organs, muscles, bones, and joints, and avoiding diseases and health conditions that can impact physical health.

- Nutrition: A balanced diet is essential for physical well-being, as it provides the nutrients needed for good health and energy. A diet rich in fruits, vegetables, lean protein, and whole grains can promote physical well-being and reduce the risk of chronic diseases.

- Exercise: Regular exercise is important for physical well-being, as it promotes cardiovascular health, strengthens muscles and bones, and improves flexibility and mobility. Exercise can also enhance mental health and reduce stress and anxiety.

- Rest: Adequate rest is essential for physical well-being, as it allows the body to repair and regenerate. Good sleep hygiene, including getting enough sleep and establishing a regular sleep routine, is important for physical well-being.

- Avoidance of harmful substances: Avoiding harmful substances such as tobacco, alcohol, and drugs is important for physical well-being, as these substances can have a negative impact on physical health and increase the risk of chronic diseases.

In summary, physical well-being is essential for overall well-being and involves maintaining good physical health, having a balanced diet, engaging in regular exercise, getting adequate rest, and avoiding harmful substances. By prioritizing physical well-being, individuals can improve their quality of life and achieve their goals and aspirations.

3. **Social well-being:** Mental health can also impact social well-being by affecting an individual's ability to form and maintain positive relationships. Individuals with good mental health are better able to communicate effectively, build social support networks, and engage in social activities, all of which can contribute to social well-being.

Social well-being refers to the state of being in positive and meaningful relationships with others, and having a sense of belonging and connection to one's community. It is an important component of overall well-being and can have a significant impact on an individual's mental and physical health.

Factors that contribute to social well-being:

- Social support: Social support is a key factor in social well-being, as it involves having access to people who can provide emotional and practical support, advice, and guidance during times of stress or difficulty.

- Communication: Effective communication is important for social well-being, as it involves expressing oneself clearly and listening actively to others. Good communication skills can enhance social relationships and prevent misunderstandings and conflicts.

- Sense of belonging: A sense of belonging is important for social well-being, as it involves feeling connected to one's community and being part of a group with shared values and interests.

- Positive relationships: Positive relationships involve mutual respect, trust, and empathy, and contribute to social well-being by providing a sense of support, belonging, and connection.

- Participation in social activities: Engaging in social activities such as volunteering, participating in community events, and spending time with friends and family can promote social well-being by providing opportunities for connection and engagement.

In summary, social well-being is an essential component of overall well-being and involves social support, effective communication, a sense of belonging, positive relationships, and participation in social activities. By prioritizing social well-being, individuals can improve their mental and physical health, enhance their sense of connection and belonging, and live a more fulfilling and meaningful life.

4. **Occupational well-being:** Mental health also plays a crucial role in occupational well-being. Good mental health can enhance an individual's productivity, job satisfaction, and overall success in the workplace.

Occupational well-being refers to the state of being satisfied and fulfilled with one's work or career, and having a sense of purpose and meaning in one's professional life. It is an important component of overall well-being, as work often takes up a significant amount of an individual's time and energy.

Factors that contribute to occupational well-being:

- Job satisfaction: Job satisfaction involves feeling fulfilled and satisfied with one's work, and having a sense of accomplishment and pride in one's achievements.
- Work-life balance: Achieving a balance between work and personal life is important for occupational well-being, as it allows individuals to pursue their interests and responsibilities outside of work, and avoid burnout and stress.

- Career growth and development: Having opportunities for career growth and development can enhance occupational well-being, as it allows individuals to develop new skills, take on new challenges, and achieve their professional goals.

- Positive work environment: A positive work environment, characterized by supportive colleagues, effective communication, and a sense of teamwork, can contribute to occupational well-being by reducing stress and promoting job satisfaction.

- Meaningful work: Engaging in work that is meaningful and aligned with one's values and interests can enhance occupational well-being, as it provides a sense of purpose and motivation.

In summary, occupational well-being is an essential component of overall well-being and involves job satisfaction, work-life balance, career growth and development, a positive work environment, and meaningful work. By prioritizing occupational well-being, individuals can achieve greater satisfaction and fulfillment in their work, and enjoy a more balanced and meaningful life.

5. **Spiritual well-being:** Mental health can also impact spiritual well-being, which refers to an individual's sense of meaning, purpose, and connection to something greater than themselves. Good mental health can enhance spiritual well-being by promoting feelings of hope, optimism, and gratitude.

Spiritual well-being refers to the state of being connected to something greater than oneself, and having a sense of purpose, meaning, and inner peace. It is an important component of overall well-being, as it involves a sense of belonging and connection to the world around us.

Factors that contribute to spiritual well-being:

- Beliefs and values: Having a set of beliefs and values that provide guidance and meaning can enhance spiritual well-being, as it provides a framework for understanding the world and one's place in it.

- Inner peace: Achieving a sense of inner peace and calmness can promote spiritual well-being, as it allows individuals to be present in the moment and connect with their inner selves.

- Connection to nature: Connecting with nature can enhance spiritual well-being, as it allows individuals to appreciate the beauty and wonder of the natural world, and feel a sense of awe and gratitude.

- Practices and rituals: Engaging in spiritual practices and rituals, such as meditation, prayer, or yoga, can promote spiritual well-being by providing a sense of connection to something greater than oneself.

- Compassion and service: Engaging in acts of compassion and service can promote spiritual well-being by providing a sense of purpose and meaning, and allowing individuals to make a positive difference in the lives of others.

In summary, spiritual well-being is an essential component of overall well-being and involves beliefs and values, inner peace, connection to nature, spiritual practices and rituals, and compassion and service. By prioritizing spiritual well-being, individuals can achieve a greater sense of purpose, meaning, and connection to the world around them, and live a more fulfilling and meaningful life.

❖ <u>The stigma surrounding mental health</u>

Stigma surrounding mental health refers to negative attitudes, beliefs, and stereotypes that lead to discrimination and marginalization of individuals with mental health conditions. It can take many forms, including social exclusion, discrimination in employment and housing, and negative stereotypes portrayed in the media.

How stigma can impact individuals with mental health conditions:

- Fear of disclosure: Many individuals with mental health conditions may fear disclosing their condition due to the stigma associated with mental illness. This can lead to feelings of shame, guilt, and isolation, and prevent them from seeking help and support.

- Discrimination: Stigma can lead to discrimination in employment and housing, as employers and landlords may view individuals with mental health conditions as less capable or trustworthy. This can lead to financial and social difficulties, and prevent individuals from reaching their full potential.

- Lack of understanding: Stigma can lead to a lack of understanding and empathy towards individuals with mental health conditions, as others may view their symptoms as a personal weakness or character flaw rather than a medical condition.

- Reduced access to care: Stigma can prevent individuals with mental health conditions from seeking care and support, as they may fear judgment or discrimination from healthcare providers or others in their community.

- Negative stereotypes: Stigma can perpetuate negative stereotypes about mental illness, such as the idea that individuals with mental health conditions are dangerous or unpredictable. This can lead to further discrimination and marginalization, and prevent individuals from receiving the support and understanding they need.

In summary, stigma surrounding mental health can have significant negative impacts on individuals with mental health conditions, including fear of disclosure, discrimination, lack of understanding, reduced access to care, and perpetuation of negative stereotypes. It is important to address and challenge stigma in order to create a more supportive and inclusive society for all individuals, regardless of their mental health status.

Chapter 2; different types of mental illness

There are many different types of mental illnesses, each with its own set of symptoms and diagnostic criteria. Here are some of the most common types:

- ❖ **Anxiety disorders**: Anxiety disorders are characterized by excessive worry and fear, and may include generalized anxiety disorder, panic disorder, and phobias.

  Anxiety disorder is a type of mental illness characterized by excessive and persistent feelings of fear, worry, or anxiety. It is a broad category that includes several specific disorders, **including generalized anxiety disorder (GAD), panic disorder, social anxiety disorder, and specific phobias.**

  - Generalized anxiety disorder involves excessive worry and anxiety about everyday life events and activities, such as work, school, and relationships. People with GAD may feel constantly on edge, have difficulty relaxing, and experience physical symptoms such as muscle tension, restlessness, and difficulty sleeping.

  - Panic disorder involves sudden and unexpected episodes of intense fear, known as panic attacks. These attacks may involve symptoms such as rapid heartbeat, sweating, trembling, and difficulty breathing. Panic disorder can be extremely distressing and may lead to avoidance of certain situations or places.

  - Social anxiety disorder involves intense fear or anxiety in social situations, such as public speaking, meeting new people, or being observed by others.

People with social anxiety disorder may avoid social situations or experience significant distress when facing them.

- Specific phobias involve intense fear or anxiety related to specific objects or situations, such as heights, spiders, or flying. People with specific phobias may avoid the feared object or situation or experience significant distress when facing it.

Anxiety disorders can be treated with a variety of interventions, including medication and psychotherapy. Cognitive-behavioral therapy (CBT) is a common type of therapy used to treat anxiety disorders, which involves identifying and challenging negative thought patterns and behaviors that contribute to anxiety. Medications, such as antidepressants and anti-anxiety medications, can also be effective in treating anxiety disorders. It's important to seek professional help for any mental health concerns, as effective treatments are available.

❖ **Mood disorders:** Mood disorders involve disturbances in mood, such as depression or bipolar disorder. Depression involves persistent feelings of sadness, hopelessness, and loss of interest, while bipolar disorder involves alternating periods of depression and mania.

Mood disorders are a category of mental illnesses that involve disruptions in mood, emotions, and energy levels. There are several types of mood disorders, but the two most common are **depression and bipolar disorder.**

- Depression is a mood disorder characterized by persistent feelings of sadness, hopelessness, and loss of interest or pleasure in activities that were once enjoyable. Other symptoms may include changes in appetite and sleep patterns, fatigue, difficulty concentrating, and thoughts of self-harm or suicide.

- Bipolar disorder involves alternating periods of depression and mania or hypomania. During manic episodes, individuals may experience elevated or irritable moods, increased energy, racing thoughts, and impulsive behavior. During hypomanic episodes, symptoms may be similar but less severe. Bipolar disorder can be challenging to diagnose as individuals may seek treatment only when they experience depressive episodes, and manic or hypomanic episodes may be overlooked or misdiagnosed.

Treatment for mood disorders typically involves a combination of medication and therapy. Antidepressants, mood stabilizers, and antipsychotic medications may be used to manage symptoms. Therapy, such as cognitive-behavioral therapy (CBT) or interpersonal therapy (IPT), can help individuals learn coping strategies, improve communication and problem-solving skills, and develop healthy habits and routines.

It's important to seek professional help if you experience persistent changes in mood, as effective treatments are available, and mood disorders can significantly impact quality of life if left untreated.

❖ **Personality disorders:** Personality disorders are characterized by inflexible and maladaptive patterns of thinking, feeling, and behavior. Examples include borderline personality disorder and narcissistic personality disorder.

    Personality disorders are a category of mental illnesses characterized by patterns of thoughts, behaviors, and emotions that deviate significantly from societal expectations and cause significant distress or impairment. There are several types of personality disorders, and they are grouped into three clusters based on their symptoms.

- Cluster A personality disorders include paranoid, schizoid, and schizotypal personality disorders. People with these disorders may exhibit odd or eccentric behavior and have difficulty with social interactions.

- Cluster B personality disorders include borderline, narcissistic, histrionic, and antisocial personality disorders. People with these disorders may exhibit dramatic, emotional, or erratic behavior and have difficulty regulating their emotions.

- Cluster C personality disorders include avoidant, dependent, and obsessive-compulsive personality disorders. People with these disorders may exhibit anxious or fearful behavior and have difficulty making decisions or taking risks.

Personality disorders can be difficult to treat, as they are often associated with longstanding and ingrained patterns of thinking and behavior. However, psychotherapy can be effective in helping individuals with personality disorders learn coping strategies, develop healthy relationships, and improve their quality of life.

It's important to seek professional help if you experience persistent difficulties with relationships, emotions, or self-image, as effective treatments are available.

❖ **Schizophrenia**: Schizophrenia is a severe mental illness characterized by hallucinations, delusions, and disordered thinking and behavior.

Schizophrenia is a serious and chronic mental illness that affects a person's ability to think, feel, and behave clearly. It is a complex disorder that typically develops in the late teenage years or early adulthood and can have a significant impact on a person's quality of life.

Schizophrenia is characterized by a range of symptoms, including delusions (false beliefs), hallucinations (seeing or hearing things that are not there), disorganized speech and behavior, and a lack of motivation or interest in daily activities. Other symptoms may include difficulty concentrating, poor memory, and social withdrawal.

The causes of schizophrenia are not fully understood, but research suggests that a combination of genetic, environmental, and brain chemistry factors may contribute to its development. Treatment typically involves a combination of medication and psychotherapy, and early diagnosis and intervention can improve long-term outcomes.

Antipsychotic medications are commonly used to manage the symptoms of schizophrenia, and therapy, such as cognitive-behavioral therapy (CBT) and family therapy, can help individuals learn coping strategies, improve social skills, and develop a support network.

Schizophrenia is a challenging illness to manage, but with the right treatment and support, many people with schizophrenia are able to live fulfilling lives. It's important to seek professional help if you or someone you know is experiencing symptoms of schizophrenia, as effective treatments are available.

❖ **Post-traumatic stress disorder (PTSD):** PTSD is a disorder that can occur after experiencing or witnessing a traumatic event, and may involve flashbacks, nightmares, and avoidance behaviors.

Post-traumatic stress disorder (PTSD) is a mental health condition that can occur after a person experiences or witnesses a traumatic event, such as combat, sexual or physical assault, natural disasters, or accidents. PTSD can develop immediately after the traumatic event, or symptoms may not appear until months or years later.

PTSD is characterized by four types of symptoms: <u>intrusive thoughts, avoidance, negative mood and thoughts, and hyper arousal.</u> Intrusive thoughts can include distressing memories, nightmares, or flashbacks of the traumatic event. Avoidance symptoms may include avoiding people or places that remind the person of the event, or avoiding thoughts or feelings related to the event. Negative mood and thoughts can include feelings of guilt, shame, or detachment from others, and difficulty experiencing positive emotions. Hyper arousal symptoms can include feeling irritable, easily startled, or constantly on guard.

PTSD can be effectively treated with psychotherapy and/or medication. Cognitive-behavioral therapy (CBT) is a type of therapy that can help individuals learn coping strategies to manage symptoms and develop a new understanding of the traumatic event. Eye movement desensitization and reprocessing (EMDR) is another type of therapy that involves guided eye movements to help process traumatic memories. Medications such as antidepressants or anti-anxiety medications can also be helpful in managing symptoms.

If you or someone you know is experiencing symptoms of PTSD, it's important to seek professional help as soon as possible. With the right treatment and support, it is possible to manage PTSD symptoms and improve quality of life

- ❖ **Eating disorders:** Eating disorders, such as anorexia nervosa and bulimia nervosa, involve abnormal eating behaviors and may be associated with body image concerns and low self-esteem.

An eating disorder is a serious mental health condition that is characterized by a persistent and abnormal eating pattern that affects a person's physical and mental health. The three main types of eating disorders are anorexia nervosa, bulimia nervosa, and binge-eating disorder.

- Anorexia nervosa is a disorder in which individuals restrict their food intake, leading to significant weight loss and a distorted body image. Individuals with anorexia nervosa may have a fear of gaining weight, despite being underweight, and may engage in excessive exercise or other behaviors to control their weight.

- Bulimia nervosa is a disorder in which individuals binge eat and then engage in behaviors to compensate for the calories consumed, such as purging, fasting, or excessive exercise. People with bulimia nervosa may experience shame and guilt about their eating behaviors and may go to great lengths to keep their behaviors hidden.

- Binge-eating disorder is a disorder in which individuals consume large amounts of food in a short period of time, often feeling out of control during the binge. People with binge-eating disorder may feel shame or guilt after a binge, which can lead to depression and other mental health issues.

Eating disorders can have serious physical and mental health consequences, including malnutrition, dehydration, and other medical complications. Treatment for eating disorders typically involves a combination of psychotherapy, medication, and nutritional counseling. Cognitive-behavioral therapy (CBT) is a type of therapy that has been shown to be effective in treating eating disorders, helping individuals to develop a healthy relationship with food and their bodies.

If you or someone you know is struggling with an eating disorder, it's important to seek professional help as soon as possible. With the right treatment and support, recovery is possible.

❖ **Substance use disorders:** Substance use disorders involve the recurrent use of drugs or alcohol despite negative consequences, and may involve physical and psychological dependence.

Substance use disorder (SUD) is a mental health condition characterized by a persistent pattern of substance use, despite the negative consequences it may have on a person's life. Substance use disorder can involve the use of alcohol, prescription drugs, or illicit drugs, and can lead to significant physical, emotional, and social problems.

The Diagnostic and Statistical Manual of Mental Disorders (DSM-5) identifies 11 criteria for diagnosing substance use disorder, including: using larger amounts of a substance than intended, unsuccessful efforts to quit using, spending a lot of time obtaining, using, or recovering from the effects of the substance, and continuing to use despite negative consequences.

SUD can have serious physical and mental health consequences, including addiction, overdose, and increased risk of mental health conditions such as depression and anxiety. Treatment for SUD typically involves a combination of medication and therapy, such as cognitive-behavioral therapy (CBT), which can help individuals develop coping strategies and new ways of thinking about substance use.

SUD can have serious physical and mental health consequences, including addiction, overdose, and increased risk of mental health conditions such as depression and anxiety. Treatment for SUD typically involves a combination of medication and therapy, such as cognitive-behavioral therapy (CBT), which can help individuals develop coping strategies and new ways of thinking about substance use.

If you or someone you know is struggling with substance use disorder, it's important to seek professional help as soon as possible. With the right treatment and support, recovery is possible.

It's important to note that mental illnesses are complex and often co-occur with other mental or physical health conditions. It's also important to seek professional help for any mental health concerns, as effective treatments are available.

Chapter 3; Factors that affect mental health

There are many factors that can affect mental health, including:

- ❖ **Genetics**: Mental health conditions can sometimes run in families, suggesting a genetic component to some disorders.

Genetics can play a role in the development of mental health conditions. Some mental health disorders, such as schizophrenia, bipolar disorder, and major depressive disorder, have been found to have a hereditary component. This means that individuals with a family history of these disorders may be at a higher risk of developing them themselves.

Research has identified specific genetic variations that may be associated with an increased risk for mental health disorders. For example, variations in genes that regulate the neurotransmitters dopamine, serotonin, and norepinephrine have been linked to the development of depression and anxiety disorders.

However, it's important to note that genetics alone do not determine a person's mental health. Other factors, such as environment and lifestyle, also play a significant role. In fact, many mental health disorders are the result of a complex interplay between genetic, environmental, and lifestyle factors.

While genetics cannot be changed, individuals who have a family history of mental health conditions can take steps to reduce their risk of developing these disorders. This may include practicing self-care techniques such as getting enough sleep, exercising regularly, eating a healthy diet, and seeking help from a mental health professional if needed. Additionally, early intervention and treatment can help manage symptoms and reduce the impact of mental health conditions.

❖ **Environment**: Exposure to stressful or traumatic events, such as abuse or neglect, can have a significant impact on mental health.

The environment can have a significant impact on mental health. Exposure to certain stressors or traumatic events can increase the risk of developing mental health conditions such as anxiety, depression, and post-traumatic stress disorder (PTSD). Here are some ways that the environment can affect mental health:

- Childhood experiences: Adverse childhood experiences, such as abuse, neglect, or exposure to violence, can have a lasting impact on mental health.

- Social support: Having a strong social network and supportive relationships can help protect against mental health problems, while a lack of social support can increase the risk.

- Work and living conditions: Working in a stressful job, living in an unsafe or overcrowded environment, or experiencing financial stress can all negatively impact mental health.

- Traumatic events: Exposure to a traumatic event, such as a natural disaster, war, or an accident, can lead to PTSD, anxiety, or depression.

- Discrimination: Discrimination based on race, ethnicity, gender, sexual orientation, or other factors can have a negative impact on mental health.

- Substance abuse: Exposure to drugs or alcohol, whether through personal use or witnessing others using, can increase the risk of developing mental health disorders.

- Access to healthcare: Limited access to healthcare or inadequate healthcare can contribute to poor mental health outcomes.

It's important to recognize that the environment is only one of many factors that can contribute to mental health problems, and that each person's experience is unique. Seeking help from a mental health professional can be an important step in understanding and addressing the factors that may be contributing to mental health problems.

- ❖ **Lifestyle**: Factors such as poor diet, lack of exercise, and drug or alcohol use can negatively affect mental health.

Lifestyle choices can have a significant impact on mental health. Here are some ways that lifestyle factors can affect mental health:

- Exercise: Regular physical activity has been shown to have a positive impact on mental health, reducing symptoms of depression and anxiety, and improving mood and overall well-being.

- Diet: Eating a healthy, balanced diet that includes plenty of fruits and vegetables, whole grains, and lean protein can help support good mental health. On the other hand, a diet high in processed foods, sugar, and unhealthy fats may contribute to poor mental health outcomes.

- Sleep: Getting adequate sleep is essential for good mental health. Sleep deprivation can lead to mood swings, irritability, and other mental health problems.

- Substance use: Substance abuse, including alcohol and drug use, can contribute to the development of mental health disorders, including addiction, anxiety, and depression.

- Stress management: Chronic stress can contribute to mental health problems, so it's important to develop effective stress management strategies, such as mindfulness, meditation, or yoga.

- Leisure activities: Participating in enjoyable leisure activities, such as hobbies or spending time with friends, can help promote good mental health.

- Work-life balance: Balancing work and personal life is important for good mental health. Overworking, being overwhelmed with responsibilities, or lacking social support from colleagues can lead to increased stress and burnout.

Making positive lifestyle changes can have a significant impact on mental health, but it's important to remember that each person's experience is unique. Seeking help from a mental health professional can be an important step in understanding and addressing the factors that may be contributing to mental health problems.

- ❖ **Social support**: Having a strong social network and supportive relationships can help protect against mental health problems.

- ❖ **Medical conditions:** Physical health conditions can also have an impact on mental health, with some conditions increasing the risk of depression, anxiety, or other mental health conditions.

- ❖ **Trauma**: Exposure to a traumatic event, such as a natural disaster, can lead to post-traumatic stress disorder (PTSD) or other mental health condition.

- ❖ **Discrimination**: Discrimination based on race, ethnicity, gender, sexual orientation, or other factors can have a negative impact on mental health.

It's important to note that mental health is influenced by a complex interplay of many different factors, and that each person's experience is unique. Seeking help from a mental health professional can be an important step in understanding and addressing the factors that may be contributing to mental health problems.

Chapter 4; Seeking help for mental illness

Seeking help for mental illness is an important step in managing and improving your mental health. Here are some steps you can take to get the help you need:

- Talk to your doctor: Start by talking to your primary care physician or a mental health provider to get a professional assessment of your symptoms. They can help determine the best course of treatment for you, which may include therapy, medication, or a combination of both.

- Consider therapy: A licensed therapist or counselor can provide talk therapy to help you manage symptoms of mental illness. They can also help you develop coping strategies and provide support as you work through your mental health concerns.

- Seek support groups: Support groups can provide a safe and non-judgmental environment to discuss your mental health concerns with others who are going through similar experiences.

- Look into medication: Medication may be necessary to manage symptoms of mental illness. A psychiatrist can help determine if medication is right for you and can prescribe and monitor your medication.

- Practice self-care: Engage in self-care activities such as exercise, meditation, or hobbies to help manage symptoms of mental illness and improve your overall well-being.

- Utilize resources: There are many resources available for people seeking help for mental illness, including hotlines, online therapy, and community mental health clinics. Don't hesitate to reach out for help.

It's important to remember that seeking help for mental illness is a sign of strength, not weakness. It takes courage to reach out for help, but taking the first step can lead to a happier and healthier life.

❖ The different types of therapy for mental illness

There are many different types of therapy, each with its own approach and techniques. Here are some of the most common types:

- Cognitive-behavioral therapy (CBT): CBT focuses on changing negative thought patterns and behaviors to improve mental health.

- Psychodynamic therapy: Psychodynamic therapy is based on the idea that our unconscious thoughts and feelings influence our behavior, and aims to help people become more aware of these influences.

- Humanistic therapy: Humanistic therapy emphasizes empathy, personal growth, and self-acceptance, and aims to help people reach their full potential.

- Existential therapy: Existential therapy explores issues related to meaning, purpose, and the human condition.

- Gestalt therapy: Gestalt therapy focuses on the present moment and aims to help people become more aware of their thoughts, feelings, and behaviors.

- Interpersonal therapy: Interpersonal therapy is based on the idea that interpersonal relationships play a crucial role in mental health, and aims to improve communication and relationships with others.

- Family therapy: Family therapy involves working with families to improve communication and relationships.

- Art therapy: Art therapy uses art-making as a means of self-expression and healing.

- Music therapy: Music therapy uses music as a means of self-expression and healing.

- Mindfulness-based therapy: Mindfulness-based therapy incorporates mindfulness practices, such as meditation, into the therapeutic process to help people become more aware of their thoughts and emotions

❖ **Medication for mental illness**

There are many different types of medications that can be used to treat mental illness. The type of medication prescribed will depend on the specific diagnosis and symptoms of the individual. Here are some common types of medications used to treat mental illness:

- Antidepressants: Antidepressants are used to treat depression, anxiety, and other mood disorders. They work by balancing certain chemicals in the brain, such as serotonin and norepinephrine.

- Antipsychotics: Antipsychotics are used to treat schizophrenia and other psychotic disorders. They work by blocking certain receptors in the brain that are associated with psychosis.

- Mood stabilizers: Mood stabilizers are used to treat bipolar disorder and other mood disorders. They work by stabilizing the mood and reducing the frequency and intensity of mood swings.

- Anti-anxiety medications: Anti-anxiety medications, also known as anxiolytics, are used to treat anxiety disorders, such as generalized anxiety disorder, panic disorder, and social anxiety disorder. They work by calming the nervous system and reducing anxiety symptoms.

- Stimulants: Stimulants are used to treat attention-deficit/hyperactivity disorder (ADHD) and narcolepsy. They work by increasing the levels of certain chemicals in the brain, such as dopamine and norepinephrine, which are involved in attention and focus.

It's important to note that medication should always be prescribed and monitored by a qualified healthcare professional, and that it may take time to find the right medication and dosage for an individual. In addition to medication, therapy and lifestyle changes can also be effective treatments for mental illness.

Chapter 5; Navigating mental health in different population

❖ **Mental health in children and adolescents**

Mental health is an important aspect of overall health and well-being for children and adolescents. Children and adolescents can experience a wide range of mental health issues, from mild to severe. Here are some common mental health concerns in this population:

- Anxiety disorders: Anxiety disorders are the most common mental health disorders in children and adolescents. These can include generalized anxiety disorder, social anxiety disorder, panic disorder, and specific phobias.

- Depression: Depression is also common in children and adolescents, and can have serious consequences if left untreated. Symptoms may include sadness, irritability, loss of interest in activities, changes in appetite and sleep patterns, and difficulty concentrating.

- Attention-deficit/hyperactivity disorder (ADHD): ADHD is a common neurodevelopmental disorder that affects attention, impulsivity, and hyperactivity. Symptoms can include difficulty paying attention, restlessness, and impulsivity.

- Autism spectrum disorder (ASD): ASD is a neurodevelopmental disorder that affects social communication and interaction, and can also involve repetitive behaviors and interests. Symptoms can range from mild to severe.

- Eating disorders: Eating disorders, such as anorexia nervosa and bulimia nervosa, can develop during adolescence and can have serious physical and emotional consequences.

It's important to seek help from a qualified healthcare professional if you suspect your child or adolescent may be experiencing a mental health issue. Treatment may include therapy, medication, and lifestyle changes, and early intervention can improve outcomes.

❖ **Mental health in Adults**

Mental health is important for people of all ages, including adults. Mental health issues can affect anyone, regardless of their age, gender, or background. Here are some common mental health concerns that can affect adults:

- Anxiety disorders: Anxiety disorders are common in adults and can include generalized anxiety disorder, social anxiety disorder, panic disorder, and specific phobias.

- Depression: Depression is a common mental health issue in adults, and can have serious consequences if left untreated. Symptoms may include sadness, loss of interest in activities, changes in appetite and sleep patterns, and difficulty concentrating.

- Bipolar disorder: Bipolar disorder is a mental health condition that causes extreme mood swings, from periods of mania to periods of depression.

- Post-traumatic stress disorder (PTSD): PTSD can develop after a traumatic event, such as a serious accident, natural disaster, or violence. Symptoms may include flashbacks, nightmares, and avoidance of triggers.

- Substance use disorders: Substance use disorders involve the misuse of drugs or alcohol, and can have serious physical and mental health consequences.

- Personality disorders: Personality disorders are mental health conditions that affect the way a person thinks, feels, and behaves. These conditions may cause difficulties in relationships and daily life.

It's important to seek help from a qualified healthcare professional if you suspect you may be experiencing a mental health issue. Treatment may include therapy, medication, and lifestyle changes, and early intervention can improve outcomes.

❖ **Mental health in marginalized communities**

Marginalized communities, such as those who face discrimination and systemic oppression based on their race, ethnicity, sexual orientation, gender identity, socioeconomic status, and other factors, are more likely to experience mental health challenges due to the stress and trauma associated with these experiences. Here are some common mental health concerns in marginalized communities:

- Trauma: Many marginalized communities experience trauma as a result of discrimination, violence, and oppression. This trauma can lead to post-traumatic stress disorder (PTSD) and other mental health issues.

- Depression and anxiety: Discrimination and oppression can also contribute to depression and anxiety in marginalized communities.

- Substance use disorders: Marginalized communities may be more likely to experience substance use disorders as a way of coping with stress and trauma.

- Suicide: Suicide rates are higher among marginalized communities, particularly LGBTQ+ youth and Indigenous populations.

- Stigma: Marginalized communities may face additional stigma and barriers to accessing mental health care, which can contribute to untreated mental health issues.

It's important to recognize the unique challenges faced by marginalized communities and work towards addressing the systemic factors that contribute to mental health disparities. This includes increasing access to culturally competent mental health care, addressing social determinants of health, and working towards greater equity and inclusion.

Chapter 6; Maintaining good mental health

❖ **Preventive measures for mental health**

Preventive measures for mental health can help reduce the risk of developing mental health issues, or help manage symptoms before they become severe. Here are some strategies that can help promote good mental health:

- Exercise regularly: Exercise has been shown to improve mood and reduce symptoms of anxiety and depression.

- Practice stress management: Strategies like mindfulness, meditation, and deep breathing can help reduce stress and promote relaxation.

- Eat a healthy diet: A balanced diet that includes fruits, vegetables, whole grains, lean protein, and healthy fats can support good mental health.

- Get enough sleep: Adequate sleep is important for mental health, and can help reduce symptoms of anxiety and depression.

- Build social connections: Strong social connections with family, friends, and community can help reduce feelings of isolation and promote a sense of belonging.

- Practice self-care: Engaging in activities that promote relaxation and self-care, such as taking a bath, reading a book, or spending time in nature, can help reduce stress and promote good mental health.

- Seek support when needed: If you are experiencing symptoms of a mental health issue, it's important to seek support from a qualified healthcare professional.

By practicing these preventive measures, you can help promote good mental health and reduce the risk of developing mental health issues.

❖ **Reducing stress and anxiety**

Reducing stress and anxiety is important for maintaining good mental health. Here are some strategies that can help:

- Practice mindfulness: Mindfulness involves paying attention to the present moment without judgment. It can help reduce stress and anxiety by promoting relaxation and reducing rumination.

- Exercise regularly: Exercise has been shown to improve mood and reduce symptoms of anxiety and depression. Aim for at least 30 minutes of moderate exercise most days of the week.

- Get enough sleep: Adequate sleep is important for mental health. Aim for 7-8 hours of sleep each night.

- Eat a healthy diet: A balanced diet that includes fruits, vegetables, whole grains, lean protein, and healthy fats can support good mental health.

- Limit caffeine and alcohol: Caffeine and alcohol can both increase feelings of anxiety and interfere with sleep. Limit your intake of these substances.

- Practice relaxation techniques: Deep breathing, progressive muscle relaxation, and guided imagery can all help promote relaxation and reduce stress.

- Seek support: If you're experiencing stress or anxiety, it's important to seek support from a qualified healthcare professional. They can provide guidance and support in managing symptoms.

By practicing these strategies, you can help reduce stress and anxiety and promote good mental health.

❖ **Building resilience**

Building resilience is an important aspect of mental health and can help individuals cope with and recover from difficult situations. Here are some strategies for building resilience:

- Cultivate positive relationships: Strong social connections can provide support during challenging times and help individuals build resilience.

- Practice self-care: Engage in activities that promote relaxation and self-care, such as taking a bath, reading a book, or spending time in nature.

- Develop problem-solving skills: Learn to identify problems and brainstorm solutions to help overcome challenges.

- Practice mindfulness: Mindfulness can help individuals stay grounded in the present moment and reduce anxiety about the future.

- Build physical resilience: Engage in physical activity and maintain a healthy diet to support physical health.

- Seek support: Reach out to friends, family, or a qualified healthcare professional for support during difficult times.

- Foster a positive mindset: Practice gratitude and focus on the positive aspects of life to build a more positive outlook.

By practicing these strategies, individuals can build resilience and better cope with difficult situations, promoting good mental health.

In summary, mental health has a significant impact on an individual's overall well-being. Good mental health can enhance **emotional, physical, social, occupational, and spiritual well-being,** while mental health problems can contribute to a range of negative outcomes. It is therefore essential to prioritize mental health as a key component of overall well-being.

Conclusion: Mental health is a complex and multifaceted topic that requires attention and care. It is important to understand the different types of mental illnesses, the factors that affect mental health, and the resources available for those who need help. By breaking the stigma surrounding mental health and promoting education and understanding, we can work towards creating a society that prioritizes and supports good mental health.

www.ingramcontent.com/pod-product-compliance
Lightning Source LLC
Chambersburg PA
CBHW072252260726
48657CB00006BA/2433